better together*

*This book is best read together, grownup and kid.

 **akidsco.com**

a kids book about CLIMATE CHANGE

by Zanagee Artis
& Olivia Greenspan

A Kids Co.
Editor Denise Morales Soto
Designer Duke Stebbins
Creative Director Rick DeLucco
Studio Manager Kenya Feldes
Sales Director Melanie Wilkins
Head of Books Jennifer Goldstein
CEO and Founder Jelani Memory

DK
Editor Emma Roberts
Senior Production Editor Jennifer Murray
Senior Production Controller Louise Minihane
Senior Acquisitions Editor Katy Flint
Managing Art Editor Vicky Short
Publishing Director Mark Searle
DK would like to thank Chris Packham

This American Edition, 2024
Published in the United States by DK Publishing
1745 Broadway, 20th Floor, New York, NY 10019

DK, a Division of Penguin Random House LLC

A catalog record for this book is available from the Library of Congress.
ISBN: 978-0-7440-9468-8

DK books are available at special discounts when purchased in bulk for
sales promotions, premiums, fund-raising, or educational use. For details, contact:
DK Publishing Special Markets, 1745 Broadway, 20th Floor, New York, NY 10019, or SpecialSales@dk.com

Printed and bound in China

www.dk.com

akidsco.com

This book was made with Forest
Stewardship Council™ certified
paper – one small step in DK's
commitment to a sustainable future.
**For more information go to
www.dk.com/our-green-pledge**

For people who are taking their
first steps on Earth today.

In honor of those who have sacrificed in silence,
whose shoulders we stand on,
whose protest left something to fight for.

Intro
for grownups

Hi, we're Zanagee and Olivia. We wrote *A Kids Book About Climate Change* to fill a gap in how we currently speak with kids (and, frankly, grownups) about climate change.

You might already be aware that climate change is a big, overwhelming issue. Perhaps the biggest challenge humanity has ever faced. Or maybe it's all new to you.

Either way, our brains are really good at lying to us about the seriousness and urgency of this problem. Our brains do a lot of mental gymnastics to prevent us from perceiving climate change for the emergency that it is.

In this book, we have tried to overcome the ways our minds lie to us about this emergency. We wrote this book as a digestible, matter-of-fact introduction that doesn't shy away from the enormity of this challenge. To get the conversation started, or to keep the conversation going! To empower kids and their grownups to fight for a livable future now— because now is all we've got.

Ready? Let's go!

This is our planet.

Does it look small to you?

That's because it is!

Once you realize how gigantic outer space is, you can see that our planet's just a little blue dot spinning around in the universe.

A famous scientist named Carl Sagan liked to point out
something kind of awesome...

Everything that's happened to any person EVER
has happened on this little blue dot we call home:

That means that
every scientific discovery,
every historical moment,
every birthday,
every rainy day, and
every special memory you have ever had
has happened right here on planet Earth.

Isn't that incredible?!

Even though we know that we
only have one home in the universe,
we sometimes forget.

We go to school,
grownups go to work,
we play with our friends,
and our planet seems like something
we don't have to worry about.

Like there's no way that
anything could happen to it.

But that's not true.

The Earth needs us to take care of it,
just like we take care of our bodies.

But recently, we haven't been doing that.

Over the past 250 years or so,
life on Earth has changed

a lot.

Humans started experimenting with travel. Suddenly, we weren't just walking, we were traveling by train, plane, and car to discover all the different parts of our planet!

We built lots of homes, buildings, bridges, and cities.

We discovered ways to meet the basic needs of a lot of people! Like food, water, and shelter.

And we didn't stop there. We made more stuff than a person could ever need or want!

I'm sure this sounds awesome to you!
I mean, how could any of this be bad?

Well, after some time, something strange started to happen.

Earth started to get sick.

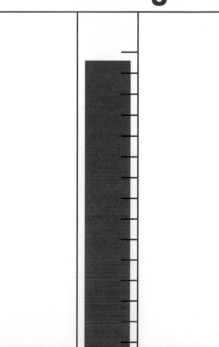

Once scientists discovered how sick our planet was becoming, leaders around the world set up laws to protect Earth.

Unfortunately, those laws have not been enough to cure Earth's illness.

Our planet has only gotten sicker and sicker.

Earth's illness is called **CLIMATE CHA**

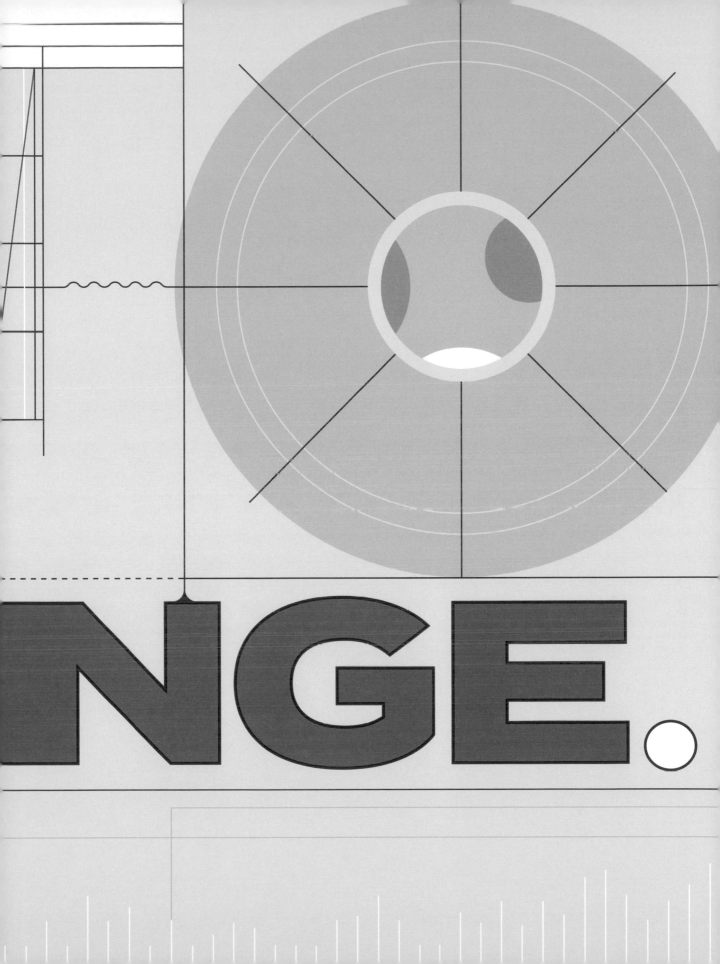

You probably know what you feel like when you're sick.

Nothing is really working right,
you can't breathe through your nose,
and can't sleep through the night!

When the Earth is sick,
it has more

floods,
fires,
droughts,
& food shortages.

This means the people who live on Earth
(that's all of us!)
may have to leave their homes,
may have trouble breathing the air outside,
and may not have access to food and water.

You can think of climate change **like the Earth getting a fever.**

Our planet is warming up kind of like how your body warms up when you have a fever.

And if you've ever had a fever,
you know how even a little one can
make a big difference in how you feel.

But wait—**why** does the Earth have a fever?

To understand that,
it's important to
understand more about

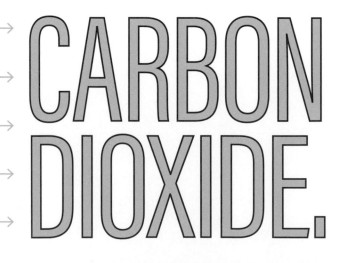

CARBON
DIOXIDE.

Too much carbon dioxide in the air is the main reason the Earth is sick.

Carbon dioxide's nickname is **CO_2** (pronounced "see-oh-two").

CO_2 has always been in our air and isn't necessarily bad.

In fact, you're breathing out CO_2 right now!

But like a lot of things in life,
too much of something can be a bad thing.

Over the past 250 years or so,
we've put a lot of carbon dioxide in the air.

A very long time ago, our planet actually had much more carbon dioxide in the air. But humans didn't even exist yet!

And Earth looked so different you wouldn't recognize it.

The seas were about 50 feet higher.

There were trees growing at the South Pole.

Can you believe it?!

Living things on our planet aren't used to CO_2 levels changing so quickly.

The more carbon dioxide we release, the sicker Earth gets, and the harder it is for humans to thrive.

Even though the Earth has only gotten sicker, our leaders have not handled the situation like an emergency.

Which isn't fair to those who didn't cause climate change—**like kids**.

What's worse is that climate change hurts some people more than others.

Confused?
Let us explain why.

Basically, the less money or resources someone has, the more they can be hurt by climate change.

For example, if

you're a young person,

you live on an island or near the coast,

you're a person with disabilities,

you're a person of color,

you don't have a home,

you're pregnant,

you're an older person...

climate change probably affects you more.

Think about it this way:

if a wildfire leaves you without a place to live, you must have the money, support, and access to resources to find a new home.

if you're a disabled person, it may be more difficult for you to leave your home if there is an emergency.

in the United States, Black families usually receive less money than white families after climate disasters and are more hurt by pollution.

These are just a few examples of the ways climate change is unfair.

You know what else isn't fair?

You didn't ask for any of this.

You didn't cause climate change.

After all...
You were born not that long ago!

But you should know that you **DESERVE** to live on our planet without having to worry about any of this.

You have a right to ─────────────

clean water.

clean air.

live on a healthy planet.

And a right is something you should **NEVER** have to worry about.

But even though you have a right to a healthy planet, not everyone is working to protect this right.

In fact, some people are fighting against it—mostly because they **make money** from making Earth sicker.

Now, after reading all of this
you're probably wondering,

"Is our planet GOING TO BE SICK FOREVER?!"

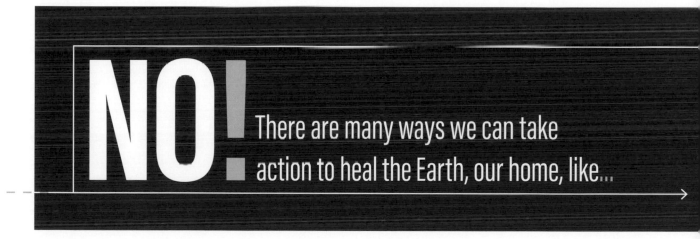

NO!

There are many ways we can take action to heal the Earth, our home, like...

Using energy from water, wind, and sun—There are no limits on how much we can use of each!

Did you know the sun provides more energy in 1 hour than the amount we need to power the Earth for an entire year?

Protecting the rights of Indigenous Peoples!*

5% ―

50% ―

― 80% ―

Did you know Indigenous Peoples are less than **5%** of the global population and protect **80%** of life on earth?

*Indigenous Peoples are the earliest known inhabitants of a place. When their rights are protected, the Earth is protected.

Educating women!

Did you know that educating women is one of the top 10 solutions to solving the climate crisis? Look it up—it's true!

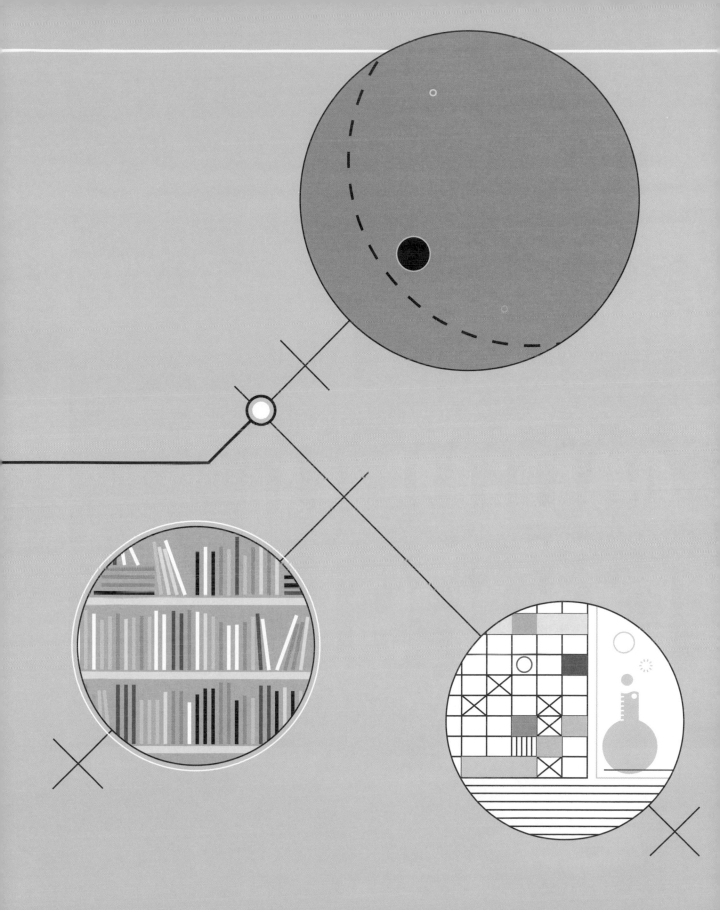

Inventing new technologies that don't hurt the planet!

Growing our food in ways that help us take carbon dioxide out of the air!

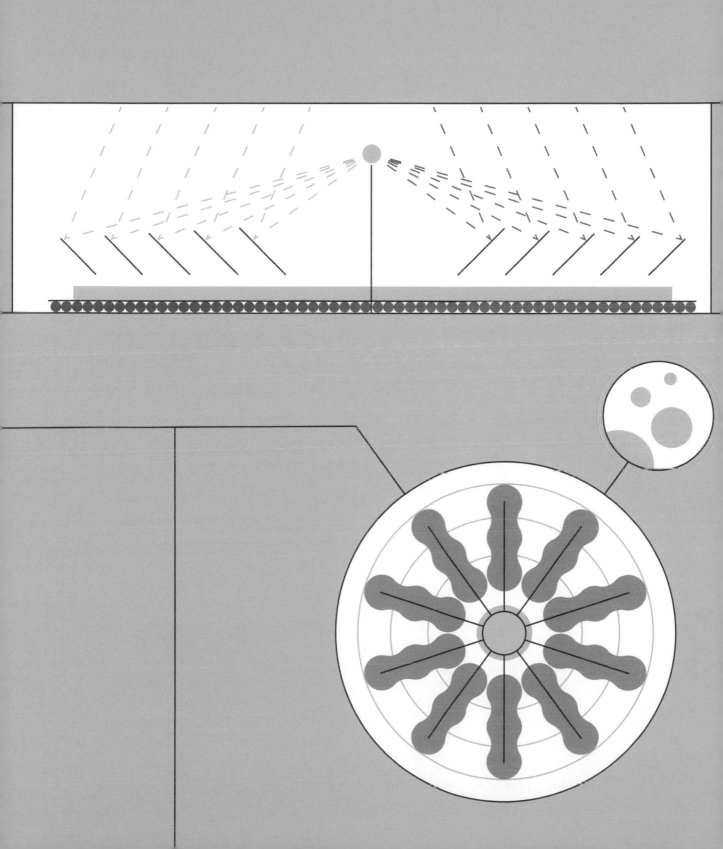

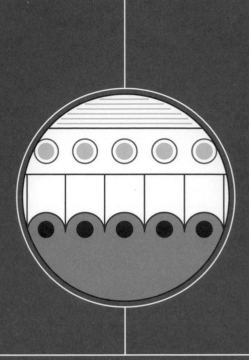

Protesting together and talking about climate change a lot, to show our leaders how much we care about making Earth healthy.

And inviting our friends to raise their voices with us.

We need everyone's special skills to help fix this problem.

Picture it!

A healed Earth...

What would that world look like?

Well, the possibilities are endless!

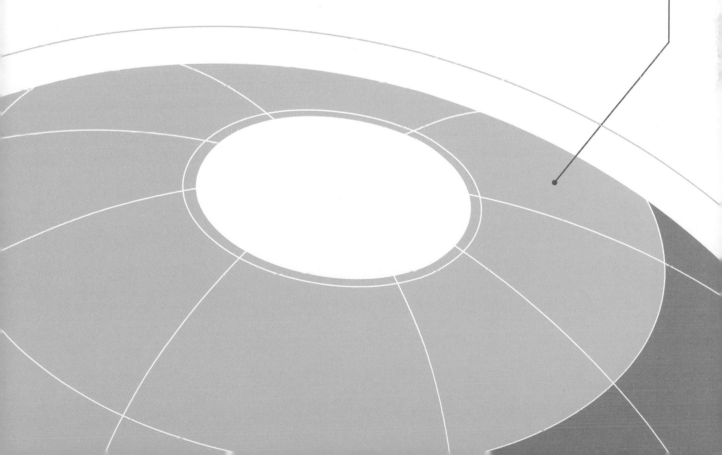

It would look like trains that can travel at SUPER FAST SPEEDS!

(Which means people could drive and fly less.)

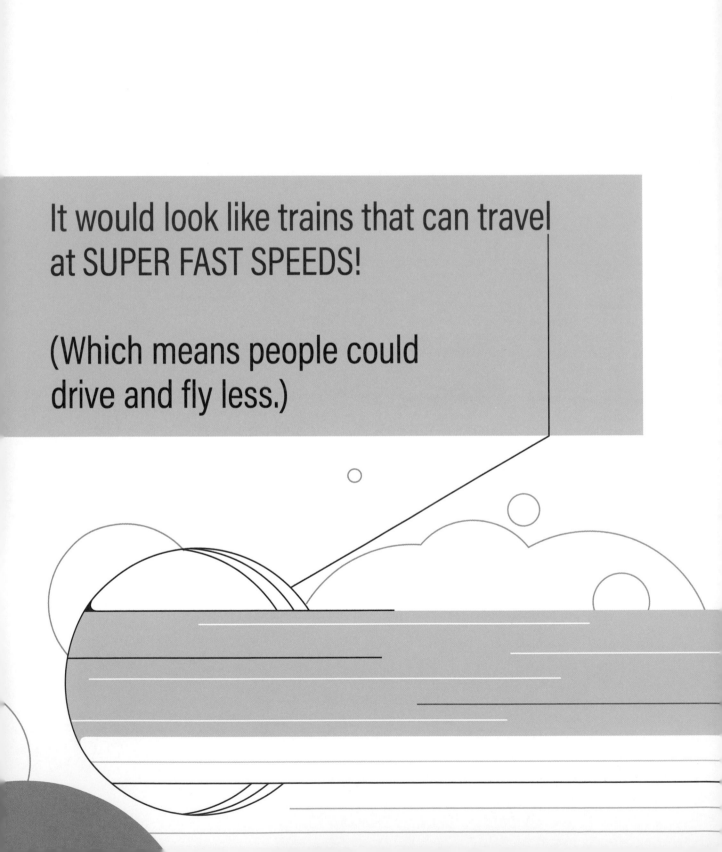

It would look like food that makes you healthier and stronger!

It would look like clothes that turn back into soil after you outgrow them!

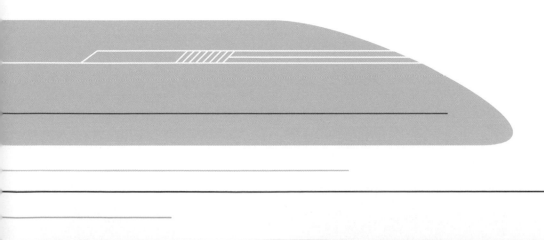

Luckily, there are many people already working on this future ——————————

AND WE NEED YOU!

No one should be born on a sick planet.

That may be the case now,
but it doesn't have to be.

A better future is possible!

**Together, we can heal our little blue dot—
our one home in the big universe.**

Outro
for grownups

Now you know what climate change is and how we got here. You know that humans are at the center of this crisis and that other big issues (like racism, sexism, and wealth inequality) are tied to climate change. It's a serious topic and there's so much more to learn than what we've shared in this book.

After reading, the kids in your life will probably have a million questions! Like, "What can our family do to fix Earth's illness?" or "Is climate change going to hurt me?" First, you should know that it's normal to experience hard emotions like grief, anxiety, or anger alongside feelings like empowerment and hope when talking about climate change. When you're ready to continue the conversation (and we hope you do!), we know it may be instinctual to talk to kids about familiar concepts like recycling, and that's great. But unfortunately, recycling is not the solution to this crisis—let's think BIGGER!

What rights do we have now because of past social movements? What unique capabilities do the kids in your life have, and how might those contribute to the climate justice movement?

We acknowledge the courage it took to read this book. So take a breath, and remember: the best antidote for climate anxiety is action.

About The Authors

Olivia and Zanagee met as college students studying climate change. Growing up on the Connecticut shoreline, Zanagee (he/him) had a deep connection to the ocean, but was unaware of the impacts climate change could have on coastal communities and marine ecosystems. Meanwhile, Olivia (she/her) felt like the environmental education she received focused too often on topics like recycling and not enough on the realities of how climate change is affecting our planet and all those who share it.

Zanagee and Olivia hope this book fills a gap in environmental education for young people. They believe children are capable and deserving of an education that addresses the many complexities of climate change. Most of all, they know kids are ready to understand how climate change is affecting the world in which they will grow up.

 @thisiszerohour   thisiszerohour.org

FURTHER READING

IPCC Global Warming of 1.5 ºC

Project Drawdown

Dumping in Dixie
by Robert D. Bullard

Pale Blue Dot: A Vision of the Human Future in Space
by Carl Sagan

Drawdown: The Most Comprehensive Plan Ever Proposed to Reverse Global Warming
Edited by Paul Hawken

A Planet to Win: Why We Need a Green New Deal
by Kate Aronoff et al.

Carolyn Merchant. 2003.
"Shades of Darkness: Race and Environmental History."
Environmental History. 8(3): 380-394.

On Fire: The (Burning) Case for a Green New Deal
by Naomi Klein

H.Res.109 -
Recognizing the duty of the Federal Government to create a Green New Deal

"Which came first, people or pollution? A review of theory and evidence from longitudinal environmental justice studies."
Environmental Research Letters by Paul Mohai and Robin Saha. 2015.

Children's Fundamental Rights and Climate Recovery Resolution or Juliana v. U.S.

Youth to Power: Your Voice and How to Use It
by Jamie Margolin

Video: A Message From the Future With Alexandria Ocasio-Cortez
by Molly Crabapple

An Indigenous Peoples' History of the United States
by Roxanne Dunbar-Ortiz

All Our Relations: Native Struggles for Land and Life
by Winona LaDuke

Braiding Sweetgrass: Indigenous Wisdom, Scientific Knowledge, and the Teachings of Plants
by Robin Wall Kimmerer

"Examining the Oil Industry's Efforts to Suppress the Truth about Climate Change."
House Committee on Oversight and Reform
(U.S. Government Publishing Office, October 23, 2019)

Made to empower.